Baby Polar Bears' Snow-Day

Parent's Introduction

This book can be read with children in several different ways. You can read the book to them or, depending on their ability, they may be able to read the book to you. You can also take turns reading! Throughout the book you will find words and phrases in big, bold text. If your child is just beginning to read, you might want to invite your child to participate in reading this text.

Your child may enjoy several readings of this story. With each reading, your child might see or focus on something new. As you read together, consider taking time to discuss the story and the information about the animals. At the end of the story, we have also included some fun questions to talk over together.

Baby Polar Bears' Snow-Day
A Photo Adventure™ Book

Author	Michael Teitelbaum
Editor	Elizabeth Bennett
Publishing Director	Chester Fisher
Art Director	Sumit Charles
Designers	Joita Das and Rati Mathur
Project Managers	Ravneet Kaur and Shekhar Kapur
Art Editor	Sujatha Menon
Picture Researcher	Shweta Saxena

Picture Credits

t=top b=bottom c=centre l=left r=right m=middle
Front Cover: John Schwieder / Alamy ; Back Cover: Steven J. Kazlowski / Alamy ; Half Title: Juniors Bildarchiv / Alamy
3 : Richard H Smith/ Photo Researchers/ Photolibrary; 4 : Suzi Eszterhas/ Nature PL; 5 (Inset): Steven Kazlowski/ Photolibrary;
6 : Blickwinkel / Alamy ; 7 : Ken Graham/ Getty Images ; 8-9 : Steven J. Kazlowski / Alamy ; 10 : Alaska Stock; 12 : John
Schwieder / Alamy ; 13 (Inset): Arco Images GmbH / Alamy; 14 (Inset) : Steve estvanik/ Shutterstock ; 15: Japan Travel
Bureau Photo/ Photolibrary; 16 : Steven J. Kazlowski / Alamy ; 18-19 : Steven J. Kazlowski / Alamy ; 20 : Alaskastock ; 21
(Inset) : Steve Bloom Images / Alamy ; 22 : Robert Harding Picture Library Ltd / Alamy ; 24 Steven J. Kazlowski / Alamy;

Published by
Treasure Bay, Inc.
P.O. Box 119
Novato, CA 94948 USA

PRINTED IN SINGAPORE

Library of Congress Catalog Card Number: 2008934734

Hardcover ISBN-10: 1-60115-281-7
Hardcover ISBN-13: 978-1-60115-281-7
Paperback ISBN-10: 1-60115-282-5
Paperback ISBN-13: 978-1-60115-282-4

Visit us online at:
www.TreasureBayPublishing.com

PR 02/10

It is cold and snowy in the frozen Arctic. What animals live here?

3

This animal lives here. It's a

polar bear!

What a long, cold winter it has been. But something wonderful has happened.

FACT STOP

Polar bears spend the winter in a den.

Two baby polar bears were born!
They are twins. There is one
boy and one **girl.**

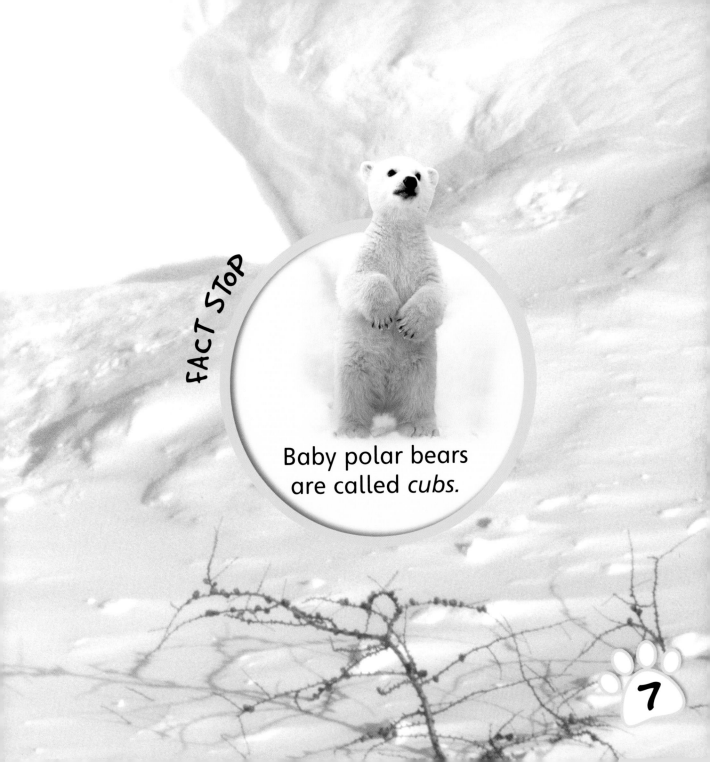

Baby polar bears
are called *cubs*.

7

Spring is here!

The **cubs** are ready to leave the den for the first time.

The baby polar bears are excited. They can hardly wait!

Look at all the snow!

The baby polar bears love
to play in the snow.

They **play** close
to their mother.

They roll and tumble!

They **slip** and **slide!**

FACT STOP

Polar bears stay warm
with a big layer of fat
called *blubber.*

13

There is so much to see!

Look at the **baby** seal on the ice.

14

Look up!

See the birds **fly** in the sky!

The baby polar bears
love to chase each other.

They **run fast**

through the snow.

The baby polar bears stop to rest.

Oh, no! Where is their mother?

They cannot **see her** anywhere.

The baby polar bears are lonely and they are very hungry.

They want some **food.**
Will they find their mother?

FACT STOP

Baby polar bears drink milk and eat fish and seal meat.

Here she is!
Their mother was right around the corner.

Now the family is all together again.
Hurry home, baby polar bears.

This has been a very busy **day!**

Look back

through the story:

1 What are baby polar bears called?

2 Why are baby polar bears so excited about spring?

3 What are some ways that baby polar bears like to play?

4 In the story, the baby polar bears are twins. What do you think it would be like to have a twin?